Landguard For

Paul Pattison

Introduction

An artillery fort on Landguard Point guarded the east coast port of Harwich for over 420 years, ever since Henry VIII personally inspected the sheltered haven. The town of Harwich played an important role in trade while also forming a base for British naval operations, notably in the Dutch wars of the late 17th century but also during the two world wars of the 20th. In 1667, an assault on the fort by Dutch marines was defeated by Captain Nathaniel Darell and the Lord High Admiral's Regiment, later the Royal Marines. The haven also witnessed the surrender of the German submarine fleet in 1918 and played host to Royal Navy ships which patrolled a vital convoy route in the Second World War.

The fort protected the haven against enemy warships. It dates partly to the mid-18th century, but includes major changes made in the Victorian period and interior fittings and smaller buildings installed by 20th-century garrisons. The pentagonal fort wall was finished about 1750: three sides survive, together with four arrowhead bastions at the corners. In the 1870s, part of the old fort was replaced by a battery of powerful guns in bombproof rooms, protected by a massive granite face and thick iron shields. A replica of one of these colossal guns, weighing 38 tons, is on display. New barracks were built around a central parade ground, and the old bastions were modified for more powerful guns.

Harwich Bastion affords a fine view of the modern container Port of Felixstowe and the whole haven, still bustling with international shipping.

Above: 17th-century trade tokens commemorating the Dutch assault on Landguard Fort in 1667. The inscription 'Poynt Fort' is an abbreviated form of Landguard Point Fort

Facing page: The 1870s casemated battery (right) and its caponier (left). Behind are the twin director towers of Darell's Battery, built in 1939–40

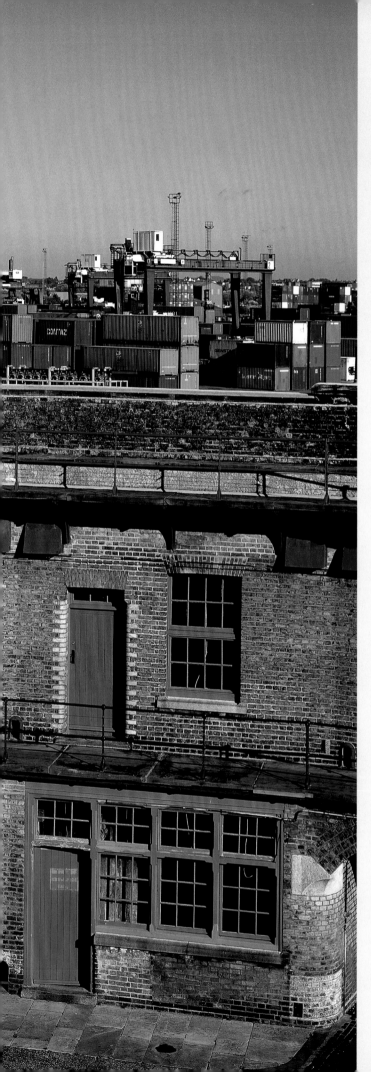

The Tour

Today, the approach to Landguard Fort is dominated by the container stacks and dinosaur-like cranes of the Port of Felixstowe. In the 18th century, there was only a windswept peninsula of flat marshland and shingle, which at high tide might be flooded, leaving the fort on a temporary island. The fort's main links were by boat to Harwich on the other side of the haven.

FOLLOWING THE TOUR

The tour visits the 18th-century outer defences of the fort before exploring the interior, including the huge elliptical keep added in the 1870s. The numbers beside the headings highlight key points on the tour, and correspond with the small plans in the margins.

◼ THE BASTIONED DEFENCES

It is possible to view the exterior defences of the fort by returning to the car park. The fort's defensive perimeter was completed in about 1750, but much of the interior results from modifications in the 1870s. The 18th-century defences comprise a pentagonal curtain wall, with bastions projecting at the corners, and a broad, flat and dry ditch. Bastions had appeared in Italy by 1500 in response to the development of gunpowder artillery which could pulverise the high walls and towers of medieval defences. The low-profile bastions and curtains like those at Landguard presented a more difficult, robust target. The bastions were carefully designed with two short flanks and two longer faces; the flanks allowed defensive fire along the curtain walls and faces of adjacent bastions to prevent an assault, while the faces allowed longer range artillery fire. Moreover, the geometry of the bastion system enabled an attack on one point to be met by defensive fire from several others. It became very elaborate, with fortifications comprised of multiple lines and tiers of curtain walls and bastions, engineered to bring massive firepower to bear against an attacking force.

The 18th-century defences here were more elaborate than they appear today. Beyond the ditch, a low earthwork rampart, the glacis, encircled the fort, incorporating a timber palisade for infantry to defend the approaches. Behind the palisade, a track called the covered way enabled any point on the perimeter to be reinforced in safety. The glacis was carefully shaped so that anyone trying to cross it was always exposed to fire from the main curtain.

Ground floor

Below: King's Bastion, built about 1750 and modified for new armament in the 1870s
Bottom: Landguard Fort from the air. The angular outline of the bastioned fort of 1750 contrasts with the curve of the 1870s casemated battery

Facing page: Accommodation for officers and men in the 1870s keep

❷ GATEHOUSE AND GUARD ROOM

The bridge across the moat included a drawbridge, from which the pulley wheels and securing rings are visible today. The cream brick facade, a decorative addition of the 1870s, is placed centrally along the East Curtain, which was covered by defensive fire from Chapel and Holland Bastions. The front of the gatehouse is in 18th-century red brick while the rear is in yellow brick of the 1870s. The passageway is paved with wooden blocks to deaden the clatter of boots and wheels. All traffic was supervised by the fort guard, typically 12 men commanded by a sergeant, who maintained a 24-hour watch.

The guard room dates from the 1870s. Its roof is carried on steel joists between shallow arches, a form of bombproof

Top: The main entrance to the fort
Above: The clock face on the rear of the gatehouse
Right: The 18th-century red-brick casemates (left) contrast with the yellow brick of the 1870s gatehouse (right)

and fireproof construction. The interior retains several fold-down beds for the use of the guard on duty, a concrete base for a stove to provide warmth in winter, and rifle racks of First or Second World War date. The adjacent small cell accommodated soldiers for short periods following minor breaches of discipline, the most common being drunkenness. The strong door has a spy hole for the guard to check the occupants and a hatch for food and drink.

Ground floor

3 4 EAST AND NORTH CURTAIN CASEMATES

The entrance passage leads to the outer parade. Looking back at the gatehouse, the guard room is to the right of the arch and the cook house to the left. The clock above the gate is a reminder of a soldier's routine, chimed out by the hour. On each side of the gatehouse, the red brick of the 18th-century East Curtain contrasts with the yellow of the 1870s gatehouse. The curtain protected round-vaulted, blind-ended rooms called casemates, which extended around the whole perimeter in the 18th century. They were used for storing ammunition, food, straw and other items, and as workshops, for example for the shoemaker, tailor and armourer. The casemates in the North and East Curtains have been re-used many times and the surviving fittings are of the late 19th and 20th centuries. To the left (north) of the gatehouse, two casemates contain bathtubs and washbasins from the first half of the 20th century. Others contain a fire engine, a store for the straw used to stuff the soldiers' mattresses, and a cobbler's workshop: good boots were a vital part of the soldier's equipment.

Below: Cobbler's equipment in one of the North Curtain casemates
Bottom: A late 18th-century drawing of the fort interior by Francis Grose, looking across the parade to the South-east Curtain casemates. The barracks (right) did not survive the 1870s remodelling, though part of the gatehouse (left) did

5 SALLY PORT

In the centre of the North Curtain is the entrance to a passage which leads under the curtain to a small but strong gate, the sally port. This could be opened when the fort was attacked, to allow a small party of defending troops to mount a surprise attack.

The Submarine Mining Establishment

The service expanded in the late 19th century until hundreds of regulars and local volunteers were employed in maintaining large underwater minefields

Coastal defences grew increasingly sophisticated during the Victorian era. In addition to more powerful artillery, underwater weapons including torpedoes and explosive mines were deployed to protect harbours from hostile warships. Effective submarine mines were first used in the Crimean War (1854–6) and from 1863 were developed in British installations worldwide. Special Submarine Mining units of the Royal Engineers were trained from 1871, the service expanding until hundreds of regulars and local volunteers were employed in maintaining large underwater minefields. The Navy took over responsibility in 1907 and continued mining operations until the end of the Second World War.

In 1877–80, a Submarine Mining Establishment (SME) was built in a new compound on the fort's northern outworks. The SME comprised a main building (the Ravelin Block) and several ancillary structures. It quickly expanded into another compound so that the volatile explosives (called guncotton) were a safe distance from the offices, stores and workshops.

Mines were transported on a narrow-gauge tramway from the SME to a jetty where a specially adapted boat awaited. The boat deployed the mines in a network of known positions in the estuary, either on the seabed (ground mines) or attached to cables to float at a given depth (electro-contact mines). Both types of mine were connected via an electric cable to a test room in the fort. An observer in a small room at roof level could track a ship using a range-finding telescope passing over a chart on which the positions of the mines were located with electrical points; when the rangefinder aligned with the target and passed over a point, the mine could be detonated. An electro-contact mine worked when a vessel hit it, tripping an electric circuit through the cable that set off an alarm bell in the test room. There the crew could explode it by a return signal on advice from the observer. Circular or barrel-shaped mines holding 100lb (45kg) of guncotton could inflict serious damage on a warship.

Below: A buoyant electro-contact mine, on a track ready to be taken to sea
Below right: The submarine mining vessel General Skinner *carrying two 500lb buoyant mines, about 1900*

6 HARWICH BASTION

Steps lead up from the outer parade into Harwich Bastion, modified for new artillery in the 1870s. In the 18th century it had a parapet pierced by openings for smooth-bore artillery mounted on wheeled wooden carriages. The visible fixings were for a rifled muzzle-loading (RML) gun of 9-inch calibre, which fired over the parapet. The gun was mounted on an iron platform which pivoted around an old gun barrel anchored in a granite bed, and moved on small wheels around a circular steel racer. The ringbolts in the parapet were for ropes and lifting equipment used when installing or removing the gun.

First floor

HARWICH HAVEN

Harwich Bastion affords a fine view across the haven. The water is shallow, apart from a channel deep enough for the passage of large ships. This channel determined the position of the fort, so that ships were obliged to sail very close to the guns, a great hazard for any with hostile intentions. It was only towards the end of the 19th century that fast torpedo boats of shallow draught were capable of entering the haven at any point. This led to the laying of defensive mines in the haven, stored and maintained in and around the Ravelin Block, the hexagonal flat-roofed building outside the North Curtain.

To the left is Darell's Battery, a complex of concrete buildings with two towers. It was built in 1900–1 for two 4.7-inch quick-firing (QF) guns to combat torpedo boats. Most of the buildings date to 1939–40 when the battery was rebuilt for twin 6-pounder guns, a more devastating replacement for the earlier guns. Nearby, three small concrete buildings housed searchlights used by the gunners of Darell's Battery to illuminate the sea when firing at night.

Above: Harwich Bastion, with the Ravelin Block beyond
Below: An engraving by Jan Kip of Harwich town and the haven in about 1714. The fort shown at Landguard (right) is the one that stood there between 1624 and 1717

Between the towers and the searchlights, a narrow brick-lined cutting carried a tramway on which mines were transported to a jetty where a boat waited to take them to sea.

On the opposite side of the haven is the tall spire of St Nicholas's Church in Harwich, and right of the church is the site of the 17th-century naval dockyard. Further to the right, a smaller green structure is a Martello tower at Shotley, built in about 1808 at the confluence of the Rivers Stour and Orwell. Left of the church, an area of undeveloped higher ground marks the Circular Redoubt, a large fort of the same period (see page 27), and further to the left is Beacon Hill, where defences were built successively from the 16th to the 20th century.

🟧 NORTH CURTAIN

This is an open platform with a traverse at each end, established in the 1870s. The platform supported two 8-inch RML howitzers for the short period 1898–1901. These specialised guns were to protect the beaches of the peninsula against troop landings, lobbing shells at high angles to explode at or just above ground level, scattering lethal showers of metal fragments and balls. The parapet is provided with a narrow ledge from which the gun commander could observe where his shells were landing; it also formed a firing position for infantry.

The traverses are short passageways which gave protection for the gun crews against bombardment from the flanks. They also provided safe and convenient places to store equipment and ammunition for the guns: each passage has two shallow alcoves on one side for storing side arms – the sponges, rammers and other items needed for loading and firing. On the other side are four deep recesses where small supplies of shells and cartridges were stored ready for use.

Below: An emplacement for a 64-pounder RML gun on the East Curtain. The central steps were inserted in the 20th century to allow entry to a pillbox

First floor

8 9 CHAPEL BASTION AND EAST CURTAIN

Like Harwich Bastion, this held a 9-inch RML gun. More clearly visible are the ammunition recesses, and openings on each flank which look along the North and East Curtains. They were originally much narrower, for a single rifleman, but were enlarged for machine guns in the 20th century.

The East Curtain has two emplacements from the 1870s, for guns that fired through openings now infilled by Second World War pillboxes and steps leading up to them. The steel racers for the gun platforms form semi-circular arcs for 64-pounder (8-inch) RMLs, multi-purpose weapons commonly found in Victorian forts. Between these guns a bombproof traverse over the gatehouse incorporates a passage similar to those on the North Curtain: it has two alcoves for side arms and six doors into shell and cartridge recesses. These were later converted into stores for position-finding equipment, used to provide accurate target information for the guns.

Above: The fort clock and bell in the gatehouse

Below: The gun emplacement in Chapel Bastion, showing the pivot and circular racer for a 9-inch RML gun

10 CLOCK CHAMBER

A seventh opening in the passage is the clock chamber. The clock was made in Ipswich in 1747 by Thomas Moore, probably as a special commission. It was repositioned in the new gatehouse in the 1870s and strikes on the hour, using a bronze bell made by Andreas Scalch in 1733. The bell may have come from the earlier 18th-century fort at Landguard.

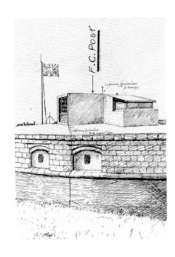

⓫ KEEP

Steps from the East Curtain descend to the outer parade near the entrance to the Victorian keep. This huge elliptical building contained a casemated artillery battery facing the haven, with barracks on the landward arc; the whole was designed as a strongpoint for a desperate final defence. The entrance incorporated a drawbridge over a deep pit and murder hole built into the top of the arch, through which the garrison could shoot down at attackers who had managed to cross the bridge.

The entrance passage opens on to the inner parade. Within the entrance range were soldiers' barracks at ground-floor level and officers' quarters on the first floor. The range opposite contains an entrance to the magazines, above which are seven arched casemates for the huge RML guns. At second-floor level is a walkway, from which the garrison could defend the keep with rifle fire and gather target information for the gun crews.

FIRE COMMANDER'S POST

The prominent L-shaped building on the roof was established in 1902–3 and enlarged in 1915. It was the control centre for all coast guns in the Harwich Command. The building contained instruments for position- and range-finding of targets, a map and chart room, a telephone room and a Port War Signal Station manned by naval personnel who monitored all ships entering and leaving the haven.

Above: A sketch dating to 1903, showing the first Fire Commander's Post on the keep roof
Below: The casemated battery and caponier, with the Fire Commander's Post of 1915 on the roof. On the outside, the caponier is protected by a massive rounded brick shield, designed to deflect incoming shells

⓬ CAPONIER

The entrance to the magazines opens into a passage that leads straight into a caponier, an enclosed defensible passage projecting from the casemated battery. This was built in the 1870s on the site of the fifth bastion of the 18th-century fort. The loopholes in the caponier enabled defenders to direct rifle fire along the ditch to prevent the wall from being scaled.

13 MAGAZINES

These rooms stored gunpowder barrels, cartridges and shells for the guns of the casemated battery, in separate rooms to minimise the risk of accidental explosion. The cartridge was a measured charge of gunpowder contained in a fabric bag, placed in the gun barrel behind the shell. Firing ignited the cartridge and propelled the shell, a pointed hollow metal casing containing its own charge, towards its target. The shell exploded and shattered when it hit the target or after an interval determined by a fuse. Solid metal projectiles, called shot, were also used.

Just inside the magazine entrance, narrow lighting passages lead to left and right, sharing a party wall with the magazines. Small glazed alcoves in the wall contained candle lanterns to illuminate the magazines safely.

The rooms to the north of the entrance stored RML ammunition. The first two rooms were for shells, and the next two for cartridges. To prevent damage to the shell casings, the floor was covered with a timber framework called skidding. Because of their great weight, shells were moved on small barrows to mechanical hoists and winched up to the guns in a protective cage. Fuses were also kept in the shell stores. Each fuse contained a small gunpowder charge which detonated to explode the shell when it hit its target or after a set time interval. The fuse was screwed into the nose of the shell immediately before firing.

The cartridges were stacked on wooden racks along the long walls of the stores, and were kept in zinc cylinders to keep them dry. Cylinders were sent up to the guns using mechanical winches similar to those used for shells.

The danger of accidental explosion was high: a simple spark from a soldier's boot might result in catastrophe. To minimise the risk, soldiers entered a shifting lobby to change from uniform and boots into special magazine clothes of finely woven cloth with no pockets, and soft slippers of leather or canvas, the object being to exclude items of metal and particles of grit – anything capable of generating friction. The lobby included a lifting wooden barrier, on each side of which were separate benches and hooks for uniform and magazine clothes.

14 THE CASEMATED BATTERY

Seven heavy RML guns – three of 10-inch and four of 12.5-inch calibre – occupied casemates of brick and concrete faced with massive granite blocks and iron shields. Each casemate was subdivided by a removable partition; the rear part was a barrack for up to six soldiers. The walls display a great variety of decorative schemes, while square concrete bases mark the sites of small stoves, which replaced Victorian originals at some time in the 20th century. Rifle brackets are of similar date, though the wall-mounted kit racks may be original.

Ground floor

First floor

Below: Making it like home: 20th-century stencilled decoration in the casemated battery
Bottom: A shell hoist and reproduction shell in the magazines

The barracks are linked through the party walls, where there are doors sealing the top of the ammunition hoists from the magazines. In action, all partitions, doors and windows at the entrance were removed to allow movement of ammunition, to prevent flying glass and wood splinters, and to help disperse the smoke generated by firing.

The front part of each casemate contained the gun. All the casemates retain their armoured shields formed by alternate layers of iron and 'iron concrete' (a mixture of asphalt, bitumen, pitch and iron). Each shield, up to 4ft (1.22m) thick, was designed to absorb the impact from a direct hit and protect the gun and its detachment of men. The steel bars around the shield supported thick rope mantlets, which were soaked in a chemical solution to prevent fire, and intended to trap shrapnel and flying masonry. On each side of the opening are small brackets for candle lamps to illuminate the gun floor, while ringbolts in the ceiling secured ropes and lifting gear for installing or removing the guns.

Below: A reconstruction of the Victorian fort in about 1880, cut away to show the caponier in the foreground, magazines and ammunition supply (left) and a 12.5-inch RML gun in its casemate

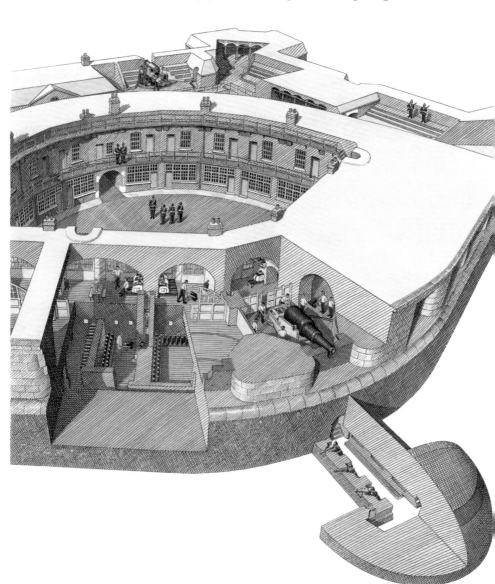

15 SEAWARD DEFENCE HEADQUARTERS

In 1952, two casemates were adapted for a new use as a Seaward Defence Headquarters from which all the coast artillery batteries in the Harwich defended area were controlled. One casemate was partitioned into four rooms – for telephones, teleprinters, a message office and wireless equipment. The second casemate contained an operations room with a platform overlooking a plotting table and radar screens.

First floor

16 17 KING'S BASTION AND SOUTH-EAST CURTAIN

The passage out of the keep is defended by armoured and loopholed doors, and by further loopholes in a flanking passage behind the adjacent walls.

King's Bastion and the South-east Curtain were converted in the 1870s for new guns on the vulnerable seaward aspect. Each casemate has a strong iron framework, to support the weight of concrete bombproofing above. The rear of each casemate was open to allow smoke dispersal. The casemate on the South-east Curtain contains a replica 12.5-inch RML and part of its traversing platform. This gun had a crew of 17 and took about five minutes to load and fire. It fired shells that could penetrate the thick armour of warships at a range of 2,000yd (1,830m) and shatter light vessels up to 4,000yd (3,660m) away. The crews worked blind, receiving target information from position-finders on the fort roof. Firing was manual or electric. In the first case, a copper tube was fitted in a small hole in the top rear of the gun barrel; it pierced the cartridge sitting in the barrel. The tube contained fine gunpowder around a friction bar, attached to a rope lanyard. The heat from the friction caused by pulling the lanyard ignited the powder in the tube and exploded the cartridge, thereby firing the shell. Electric firing replaced the lanyard with an electric current and had the advantage that the guns could be fired more rapidly on the order of the battery commander.

Below left: Replica 12.5-inch RML gun in a casemate on the South-east Curtain. This 38-ton giant loaded at the muzzle (front) and fired a shell of 818lb (371kg), using two cartridges of gunpowder weighing 80lb (36.3kg) each

Below: Armoured doors, pierced with loopholes for riflemen, separating the keep from the South-east Curtain

Life at Landguard Fort

Living conditions were poor before the 20th century: barracks were tightly packed, smelling strongly of food, smoke and sweat

Life for the garrison soldier was a mixture of routine and boredom punctuated by occasional excitement. During its 420-year military occupation, Landguard was garrisoned by all manner of soldiers. It was an isolated and lonely posting.

In the 17th century, the garrison was constantly short of supplies and pay from an impecunious government. In 1661 Colonel Henry Farre, commanding 112 men, complained of their diet of bread and cheese, and that with only 20 bedsteads, most men were sleeping on the floor.

For much of the 18th century, Landguard was manned by an Invalid Company of soldiers unfit for active service, and the guns were maintained by a Master Gunner and a few assistants. It was normal for peacetime garrisons to be under strength, and to be topped up with regular troops in wartime.

In 1850 Landguard became an artillery garrison, and by the 1870s could accommodate 83 men and four officers in 16 rooms, most of which held six men. A hundred more could be accommodated in hut barracks on Landguard Common, generally in the summer when the local militia arrived for training. At this time a soldier's day lasted from 9am until 8pm and comprised drill, guard, cleaning equipment and other mundane tasks. Only occasionally was there the excitement of firing of the guns, usually to salute a VIP arriving in Harwich, or occasionally during an exercise such as that of 1895 when a night attack was simulated.

Living conditions were poor before the 20th century. Facilities and sanitation were primitive and barracks tightly packed, often smelling strongly of food, smoke and sweat. Concern over poor conditions led to the appointment of an Army Sanitary Commission in 1857. Its reports revealed frequent squalor and overcrowding but improvements followed only gradually. The army reforms of the 1870s resulted in more frequent provision of married quarters, proper toilets, running water, washrooms and recreation rooms. Conditions for the men at Landguard were moderately good, with barrack rooms for four to six men per room.

Discipline was more relaxed in garrison than on campaign but the cell of the guard room was often occupied. Boredom led to gambling, brawling, and drunkenness, for which various punishments were inflicted, the most serious being flogging. Officers and men alike sought diversions in sport. In the late 19th century there were many attempts at diverting soldiers into 'civilised' pursuits and Landguard witnessed communal evenings of readings and songs in the recreation room. At Christmas 1882, decorations were put up and the women and children were given tea by the officers, followed by the distribution of presents around a Christmas tree in the schoolroom.

Below: Kit and rifle racks in the guard room
Bottom: 20th-century washbasins in the East Curtain casemates

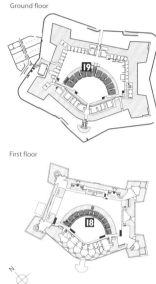

Ground floor

First floor

18 OFFICERS' QUARTERS

The rear range of the keep at first-floor level contained the officers' quarters. This comprised a suite of 13 rooms for four officers, an allocation of space and privacy which contrasts with the cramped conditions of the ordinary soldiers. Rooms 2–4 were for individual officers, while 1 and 5 were for their servants. The Field Officer in overall command had 6 and 7 and his bathroom, 8, was in the chamber which contained the murder hole over the keep entrance. Rooms 9–11 were interconnected and formed the ante-room, dining room and kitchen of the officers' mess, while 12 contained its larder and wine store. Room 13 was the officers' latrines.

Each room is similar, with a glazed wooden storm lobby, a fireplace with cast-iron surround, a ceiling ventilator, cupboards and shelves (only parts of which survive), skirting, panelling and coat hooks. Interesting features include the hatch between rooms 4 and 5, next to which is a bell pull used by the officer to summon his servant.

19 SOLDIERS' BARRACKS

Beneath the officers' rooms are ten more barrack rooms, each for six ordinary soldiers. One of these rooms is kitted out to the late Victorian period. The rooms each have a storm lobby and a fireplace. When in use, a mess table occupied the central space; the soldiers' beds had slide-under sections to maximise space during the day. Above each bed is a kit rack and to the side is a rifle bracket.

Above: The officers' quarters on the first floor, with the barracks for ordinary soldiers below
Below: A cast-iron fire surround in the officers' quarters

History

The earliest known defences at Landguard can be traced back to the reign of Henry VIII, and a fort built in the 1620s fought off a Dutch attack in 1667. The present buildings, dating from the mid-18th century onwards, remained in military use until the 1960s.

READING THE HISTORY

This section traces the history of the successive forts at Landguard and the wider defence of Harwich Haven. There are features on military engineers (page 20), the Dutch attack of 1667 (page 23), an 18th-century fort governor (page 26) and a posting to Landguard in 1939 (page 35).

HENRY VIII AND DEFENCE OF THE REALM

The first plan for protecting Harwich Haven with artillery defences evolved during the period 1539–43, when the threat of invasion from the combined forces of Catholic Europe caused frantic building of defences around the coast. South from Hull round to Milford Haven, Henry VIII constructed fortifications to prevent major harbours from falling into enemy hands. In 1539, the medieval wall of Harwich was modified by the addition of two bastions and defensive trenches. The Lord Chancellor, Thomas Audley, observed, 'Ye should have seen women and children work with shovels in the trenches and bulwarks.'

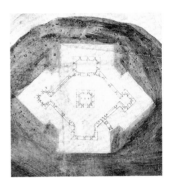

These measures were followed in 1543 by a more considered plan, after a visit by Henry himself. The king's engineers Richard Lee and Richard Cawarden spent £2,717 on five small 'bulwarks', two at Landguard and three in Harwich. These were small earthwork and timber forts with small garrisons and assorted artillery pieces; the one on Landguard Point was circular, defined by a ditch with an earth rampart on which the guns were mounted. It stood about 350m east of the present fort, a point now lost to the sea.

The deteriorating political situation of the 1580s, particularly the prospect of a Spanish invasion (the Armada), prompted further work at Harwich. In 1587–8, the Privy Council granted £1,000 as a contribution towards fortifying the town walls, including a stone bulwark to defend the haven, and repairs to the Landguard bulwarks. Some 46 cannon were mounted there.

Above: A design of about 1543 for a fortification on Landguard Point, made by Richard Lee, one of Henry VIII's engineers

Below: A late 16th-century map of Harwich Haven, showing the small artillery bulwark on Landguard Point

Facing page: On the lookout – a young gunner in the observation post of Right Battery in 1943

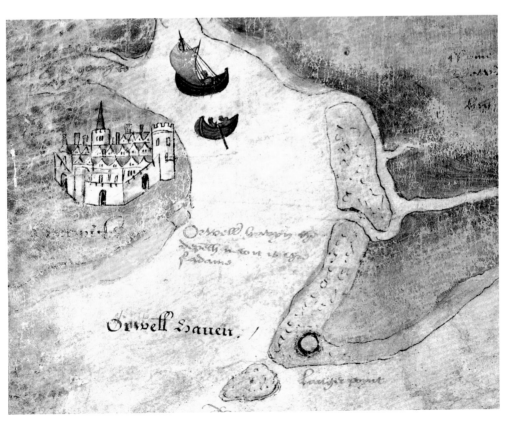

Orwell Hauen.

The Fortress Builders

Unlike infantry and cavalry officers, who bought their commissions, engineer officers were appointed on merit and from 1741 received professional training

Skilled engineers designed and built castles throughout the medieval period. During the 15th century, the architecture and technology of fortifications became a science that attracted talented professionals. In the 16th century prominent military engineers, including John Rogers and Richard Lee, were employed by Henry VIII to design and construct artillery fortifications along the east and south coasts, including those at Harwich.

By the late 17th century, the government body responsible for permanent fortifications was the Board of Ordnance, established in the early 15th century. Under the control of its Master-General, it was independent of the Army and Navy and enjoyed full control of artillery and engineers until its abolition in 1855. In 1716, the artillery and engineers were formed into the Royal Regiment of Artillery and the Corps of Engineers. Unlike infantry and cavalry officers, who bought their commissions, engineer officers were appointed on merit. From 1741, they received professional training at the Royal Military Academy in Woolwich, now in south-east London, from which many officers of exceptional talent passed out to design and build fortifications worldwide.

Fortifications at Landguard were undertaken by notable officers, including Charles II's engineer Sir Bernard de Gomme (in the 1660s) and John Peter Desmaretz who built the fort of 1750, part of which remains visible. Their colourful lives are exemplified by Lieutenant Thomas Hyde Page, who lost a leg at Bunker Hill in 1775, during the American War. Returning home, he was promoted to captain and employed as Engineer to the Eastern Coastal District. He remodelled many fortifications at a time of national emergency, including those in Dover and Chatham, Kent, on the Thames and at Landguard, and was knighted for services to the Crown.

Above: The Board of Ordnance crest, cast onto the fort clock's bell of 1733
Right: The military engineer Thomas Hyde Page, by Sir Thomas Northcote, painted c.1778–82. Landguard Fort, which Page remodelled in the 1780s (see page 25), is shown in the background, and Page is holding a plan of the fort in his left hand

DEFENDING HARWICH HAVEN IN THE 17TH CENTURY

The Landguard bulwarks were badly neglected by 1603, when the accession of James I brought peace with France and Spain. Nationwide, coastal defences were reduced but a few permanent forts were proposed at strategic locations, including Harwich, where the Half-moon Battery was built on the quayside, and Landguard, where a new fort was made. Both were constructed between 1625 and 1628. At Landguard the fort was built to a very low profile, square in plan with acute-angled bastions at each corner and a broad external ditch. The rampart and ditch were of sand and shingle revetted with sods and clay slabs. The main gate had a portcullis and led to a drawbridge across the ditch. Inside, around a small square parade ground, were brick barracks for the soldiers, a governor's lodging, magazines, an aqueduct, a conduit house for water and a chapel.

In 1627 the fort had a garrison of 77, perhaps rising to 126 in 1628, and 62 artillery pieces of various calibres. From the beginning, the annual allowance for pay and maintenance was constantly in arrears, and there was a minor mutiny in 1628. The mutiny was quickly stopped and Captain Gosnold allowed the offenders to draw lots so that only one man would be punished. The unlucky Benjamin Dammont was despatched to gaol near Woodbridge, Suffolk, but only got as

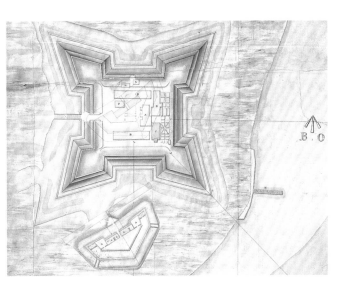

Above: A drawing of the lonely and windswept Landguard peninsula, made by Francis Place in the late 17th century. The fort is on the far right

Left: A plan of 1716 showing the outline of the 17th-century fort, with proposals for a smaller battery to replace it

Above: Dutch warships during the attack on Landguard in 1667, from a painting of 1669 by Willem Van de Velde the Elder. The fort is just visible in the distance at the centre

far as Trimley St Mary, where the village constable took pity and let him go, sending the warrant back to the fort.

Although the garrison held for Parliament throughout the civil wars of 1642–8, by 1647 official neglect had taken its toll and the defences were badly eroded from the constant assault by wind, sea and rain. A few years later, England found itself at war with the Dutch during an extended period of international trading rivalry. In three wars fought in the years 1651–4, 1665–7 and 1672–4, the waters off the east coast were the scene of many naval engagements and piracy. Harwich was vital as a safe haven for naval and mercantile vessels, and Major Nathaniel Bourne operated a small private shipyard for their repair. In 1666, it became an official naval dockyard and operated as such until 1713. Throughout these wars, Landguard Fort was the main defence for the anchorage, but in 1656 conditions had not improved and most of the men were staying with the local population at night. In 1663, orders were given for the fort to be dismantled and only the intervention of the Master-General of the Ordnance prevented its destruction. With the increasing prospect of invasion and naval attacks, many coastal forts were repaired, and in September 1666 Landguard was reinforced with a detachment of the Lord High Admiral's Regiment (the forerunner of the Royal Marines). In June 1667, the Dutch made a daring and successful attack on the English fleet in the Medway. In consequence, the authorities in Harwich made frantic preparations in anticipation of an attack which came in the following month, when the Dutch launched an assault on Landguard Fort itself. Fortunately, it was repulsed by the garrison.

Captain Nathaniel Darell and the Dutch Assault

In the 17th century, England fought three wars against the Dutch, largely over competition for trade in emerging global markets. Most of this fighting was at sea. During the St James's Day Fight in 1666, the English fleet inflicted a serious defeat on the Dutch. For the remainder of 1666 and much of 1667, the English fleet languished in port at Chatham on the River Medway in Kent, lacking money and supplies to put to sea. Elsewhere in England, tension was high in anticipation of a Dutch counter-attack. Coastal forts including Landguard were repaired and supplied, and other makeshift defences constructed.

From 10 June 1667 until the 16th, the Dutch attacked the English fleet in the Medway. With little effective resistance, they destroyed the fort at the mouth of the river at Sheerness, penetrating as far as Upnor Castle. Several English warships were burnt and two towed away as prizes, including the flagship *Royal Charles*.

The raid threw England into turmoil and on 2 July the Dutch launched an attack on Harwich. Twelve warships from the 70-strong Dutch fleet of Admiral de Ruyter attempted to bombard Landguard Fort, but the ships could not get close enough for accurate fire in the treacherous waters. A force of 800 Dutch troops made two attempts to storm the fort but they were driven back by the 200-strong garrison under Captain Nathaniel Darell, aided by cannon fire from a small warship whose cannonballs had the effect of scattering the beach shingle in deadly showers. The attackers were unable to cross the fort ditch because of the hail of musket shot from Darell's men, placed securely behind a wall at the base of the fort rampart. The Dutch retreated, leaving eight dead. Only one Englishman was killed and Darell, who sustained a slight shoulder wound, was hailed as the hero of the day.

> Dutch troops made two attempts to storm the fort but were driven back by the 200-strong garrison under Captain Darell

Above: *Admiral de Ruyter, who led the Dutch attack on Landguard in 1667, from a painting by Charles de Jardin dated 1669*
Left: *Detail from* The Dutch in the Medway 1667, *by Willem Schellinks (1627–78)*

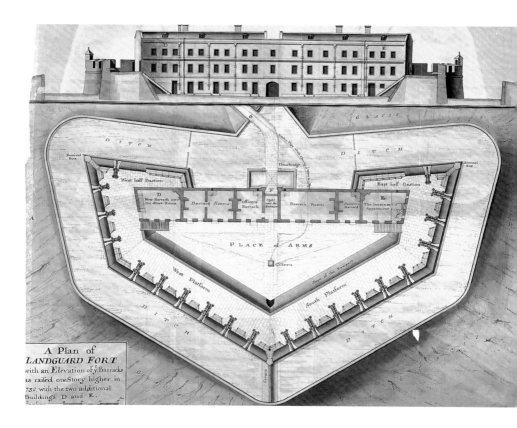

A Plan of
LANDGUARD FORT
with an Elevation of y. Barracks
as raised one Story higher in
1732 with the two additional
Buildings D and E.

Above: The fort of 1717–20, after
alterations made between 1730
and 1733

Below: A sketch of guns at
Landguard in 1711, from the
diary of James Thornhill

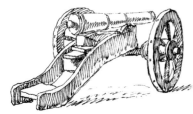

DEMOLITION, REBUILDING AND EXPANSION IN THE 18TH CENTURY

War broke out with France in the early 18th century, during which John Churchill, Duke of Marlborough, led an English field army on the continent with spectacular success. At home, measures were taken to secure the naval dockyards against attack, following an Act of Parliament in 1709. A survey by John Brookes in 1716 made it clear that the old fort at Landguard was not worth repairing, and ambitious plans for a new fort were made. These were scaled down to a small brick battery incorporating barracks for a garrison of 30, built 1717–20.

The new fort was an economic design, with two principal faces on to the haven, two short flanks and the rear closed by a defensible barrack range. The surrounding ditch was defended from casemates built behind the outer wall of the ditch and by a caponier – an enclosed defensible chamber built across the ditch. The barrack faced on to a small triangular parade ground, while the rampart supported 20 pieces of artillery, with casemates containing gunpowder underneath.

The new fort was very small because it was intended to work with new and larger fortifications in Harwich. After a decade, nothing had been done in Harwich and it was proposed to enlarge Landguard. Alterations were made there between 1730 and 1733, comprising the addition of another storey to the barracks and a larger battery of heavier guns to combat the powerful warships of the day. Against a background of war with France and the Jacobite rebellion in Scotland in

1745, the Board of Ordnance constructed a new fort at Landguard between 1744 and 1750. This incorporated the two main faces, the barrack block and the parade of the existing fort into a larger pentagonal design, with bastions projecting at the salient angles. Inside were new casemates and buildings. Beyond the ditch, an additional earth and timber rampart was built for infantry defence. On the haven side, by 1753 a new artillery battery – Beauclerk's Battery – had been built specifically to engage warships.

THE ENTRENCHED CAMP, 1779–1803

At the end of the Seven Years' War in 1763, fought across the globe mainly against the French, Britain enjoyed an era of relative peace until 1775, when conflict broke out in the American colonies. With France, Spain and the Netherlands joining the Americans, Britain's defences were stretched and invasion was feared. Improvements to coast defences became critically important. Captain Thomas Hyde Page constructed a new battery in Harwich and by 1779 had proposed a new 600-yard (550m) long entrenchment across the Landguard peninsula north-east of the fort, exploiting the area of low ground that was inundated at high tides. This would make Landguard Point into a large defended camp sheltering a mobile field force. Page refined his ideas and late in 1782 work was under way on the King's Lines and the Prince's Lines, with ramparts supporting artillery protected by an external ditch. Wing batteries were built to defend the fort's flanks and smaller redoubts (strong points) were established within the entrenched area. These works were incomplete when the war ended in 1782 and were gradually abandoned.

Above: One of the 18th-century casemates on the East Curtain
Below: The new Landguard Fort of the 1740s, detail from a landscape by Thomas Gainsborough, painted between 1743 and 1753

Philip Thicknesse, Lieutenant-Governor

'He was susceptible in the extreme of everything that bordered on insult and rudeness'

Above: A miniature painting of Philip Thicknesse by Nathaniel Hone, 1757. Despite Thicknesse's inflammable temperament, he had many admirers and his three wives adored him

Below: It was probably the eccentric Thicknesse who created the ornamental garden on the fort rampart, shown in this watercolour of the Lieutenant-Governor's house and North Curtain in 1769, just after Thicknesse's tenure

Landguard Fort attracted some notorious characters but none more so than Philip Thicknesse. Born in 1719, he left school in Westminster after repeated truancy, emigrating to America aged 16 and living 'a Robinson Crusoe type of life'. He returned in 1737 to an army commission, and his career in England, Jamaica and the Mediterranean was characterised by frequent quarrels. He made a home in Bath, where he enjoyed society, gambling and overindulgence in laudanum.

In 1753 he bought the Lieutenant-Governorship of Landguard Fort. He picked quarrels with officers and local dignitaries, in 1761 bringing a court martial against a captain not under his command, who was acquitted. Thicknesse's conduct was reprimanded by Colonel Francis Vernon, who presided at the trial. Thicknesse pursued the quarrel with Vernon and attempted to sabotage the latter's election hopes by publishing scandalous broadsheets. Found guilty of slander in August 1763, Thicknesse was imprisoned for three months. On returning to Landguard, he brought ridiculous charges against the officer who had commanded in his absence, and was himself sentenced to a public reprimand in 1765. Thereafter he was judged unfit for command and he resigned in 1766.

After 1766 Thicknesse returned to Bath; he travelled in Europe with his family and wrote several lucrative travel books. Among other bizarre works, in a guide to Bath he recommended 'drinking to excess' and 'the frequent inhalation of the breath of young women'. His quarrels were still numerous: notably he fell out with the painter Thomas Gainsborough, whom he had met at Landguard in 1754, and disowned his own two sons. He died in 1792 and his memoirs (1790) proved very popular. In 1809 the *Gentleman's Magazine* noted, 'In point of person he was extremely handsome; his conversation was entertaining, his talents undisputed ... he was susceptible in the extreme of everything that bordered on insult and rudeness.'

DEFENCE AGAINST NAPOLEON

Britain fought a bitter war with France between 1793 and 1815, mainly in continental Europe. Napoleon's armies pursued plans to invade England on three occasions: 1797, 1801 and 1803–5. The threat prompted a systematic review of defences. Areas susceptible to beach landings were to be protected by gun towers developed from prototypes used in the defence of the Channel Islands from the 1780s. In 1794, a similar tower successfully resisted warships of the Royal Navy at Cape Mortella in Corsica, from which Martello towers took their name. Following the completion of Martello towers along the south coast, 27 were built along the east coast between 1808 and 1812. Each mounted three pieces of artillery, often supported by guns at ground level nearby, and had a small garrison of an officer and 30 men.

In the scheme, Harwich Haven was defended to prevent its capture and use as a bridgehead by an invading force. In 1795, Page's infantry camp was removed from Landguard to a more secure location behind Beacon Hill in Harwich. Significant improvements to Landguard Fort included, in 1806, work at Beauclerk's Battery to give the heavy 42-pounder guns traversing carriages which enabled each gun to fire over a wider arc. By 1817, the bastions of the fort had 24-pounder guns on similar carriages. Most importantly, an entirely new fort was built in Harwich between 1807 and 1810. The Circular Redoubt was armed with ten 24-pounders that covered the town from landward assault and the haven against any ships which managed to slip past Landguard. It had an infantry garrison in bombproof barracks, which could deploy against enemy landings. It was also the command centre and support base for the other elements in the haven defences: five Martello towers, four open batteries and the large infantry corps camped on Beacon Hill.

Above: The Circular Redoubt in Harwich, built between 1807 and 1810 on a low hill to supplement the defences of the haven

Below: A Martello tower at Bawdsey in Suffolk, one of 27 such towers built along the east coast between 1808 and 1812 in response to the threat of invasion by Napoleon

VICTORIAN REBUILDING

The feared invasion never came, and with peace in 1815 defences were rapidly reduced to the minimum. However, Landguard Fort and the Circular Redoubt retained their guns and garrisons. The years to 1850 were peaceful at home but the ingrained fear of French imperialism re-emerged in the 1840s and 1850s. In 1859, a Royal Commission began to examine the defences of the United Kingdom against a background in which major technological developments were transforming warfare. The building of fast steam ships with hulls protected by iron plate and which carried new and powerful rifled guns posed a great threat to existing coastal forts. The Royal Commission report of 1860 recognised that defences had to be radically changed to match these threats, and there followed the greatest period of fortress building ever witnessed in the British Isles.

There was no new work at Landguard immediately after 1860. Instead, the other haven defences were upgraded, with new guns for four Martello towers and the Circular Redoubt. An entirely new battery was built at Shotley Point, for fourteen 68-pounder guns, by 1863. Landguard Fort remained seriously neglected, partly because of a belief that Shotley Point could command the entire haven, making Landguard and the other defences superfluous. Dissenting voices gained the upper hand following the failure of the French fixed defences during the Franco-Prussian War of 1870–1, and new work at Landguard was approved.

From 1870 to 1878, the west and south-western parts of the old fort were demolished and replaced with seven huge rifled muzzle-loading guns (RMLs) in a curved casemated

Above: Queen Victoria's initials above the entrance to the keep
Below: The keep and inner parade, showing one of the gun casemates (left) and the soldiers' barracks and officers' quarters (right)

battery. The old internal buildings were replaced by a semi-circular barrack that broadly mirrored the shape of the new battery and which could itself be defended from land attack. The rest of the old fort – rampart and four bastions – was remodelled for a further nine RMLs, two in casemates, the others in open positions on the rampart. Work was almost but not entirely finished by 1886, once more overtaken by technological change. At this date, the fort could house 98 officers and men, with extra accommodation in the hut barracks, built outside in 1872–3. These were improved and extended such that, by 1896, there was permanent accommodation at Landguard for 200 officers and men.

THE RESPONSE TO NEW THREATS, 1880–1905

Towards the end of the 19th century, technology continued to revolutionise warfare so that static defences proved vulnerable to the power of new guns and faster warships. At the same time, electricity and telephones brought faster communications and influenced tactics, while the use of concrete enabled more rapid construction of defences to new designs. Even as they were being installed, the Army realised that Landguard's RMLs were too heavy and slow to be effective.

One solution came in the form of new breech-loading (BL) guns which fired shells further and more accurately. These guns were mounted to enable quicker firing and better control of recoil. In the 1850s, Captain Moncrieff developed guns whose barrels were elevated over a parapet to fire and retracted into the safety of a deep gun pit for reloading. This idea was modified in the 1880s so that, on firing, recoil caused the gun barrel to pivot down into the gun pit where it was

Above: One of the iron gun shields set in the granite face of the casemated battery
Below: A late 19th-century drawing of a 6-inch breech-loading (BL) gun on a 'disappearing' carriage

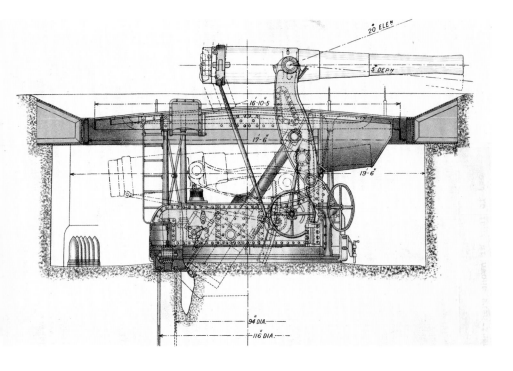

Above: Reconstruction showing Landguard Fort and its batteries as it would have appeared in about 1904

secured for reloading. The excess energy of recoil was stored as hydro-pneumatic pressure which, when the barrel was released, caused it to return to the firing position. These 'disappearing' guns were placed in small batteries intended to be 'invisible', protected by concrete emplacements fronted by a sloping bank of earth or sand to absorb incoming fire, with underground ammunition stores. In 1889–90, 'disappearing guns' of 10-inch and 6-inch calibres were installed in Left Battery outside Landguard Fort and at Beacon Hill in Harwich, for rigorous service testing.

By 1900 a new form of mounting came into use, in which the barrel recoiled along its axis and was mounted permanently over a low parapet. Guns of this type, even quicker to load and fire, were installed in 1898–1902 at Landguard Right Battery (two 6-inch and one 10-inch BL). Minefield Battery was built outside Landguard Fort in 1900–1, and equipped with two 4.7-inch quick-firing (QF) guns for the protection of the submarine minefield against fast torpedo boats. It was soon renamed Darell's Battery after the hero of 1667.

Along with new guns came improvements in command and control. From the 1880s, powerful electric lights allowed firing at night, while new position- and range-finding instruments enabled more accurate fire. By 1903, a formidable system of defence protected the haven. It was curtailed in 1905 by the government Committee on the Armaments of the Home Ports, whose report recommended the grading of ports according to the likelihood of attack, with defences allotted proportionately. Harwich received a low grading and its 10-inch guns were removed. By 1910, the haven defences were concentrated at the entrance and comprised the submarine minefield and the 6-inch and 4.7-inch guns at Landguard and Beacon Hill.

THE FIRST WORLD WAR, 1914–18

When war came in 1914, the risk of invasion led to the designation of Harwich both as a War Anchorage for the Royal Navy and a Class 'A' fortress. This involved the construction of extensive land defences, comprising trenches, barbed-wire entanglements, pillboxes and earthwork redoubts across the Harwich and Dovercourt peninsula, and around Landguard and Felixstowe. The new threat from airships and aeroplanes required anti-aircraft guns at Walton Martello tower, Landguard Right Battery, Landguard Common and Harwich.

As Harwich was a naval base used by destroyers and other vessels, entry to and exit from the haven were strictly controlled from a Port War Signal Station. This was incorporated into the Fire Commander's Post on the roof of Landguard Fort, housing naval personnel equipped with semaphore to challenge every vessel for the correct signal, monitored by the 6-inch guns of Right Battery. The submarine minefield remained in place.

The threat from enemy warships required the return of heavy guns similar to those withdrawn in 1905. Accordingly, a battery was built in 1915 at Brackenbury, at the northern end of Felixstowe, for two 9.2-inch BL guns. These, and the 6-inch and 4.7-inch guns at Landguard and Beacon Hill, were manned continuously throughout the war.

A seaplane base on the haven was established in 1913. By 1915, at Royal Naval Air Station (RNAS) Felixstowe, large seaplane sheds were under construction and thereafter seaplanes were engaged in anti-submarine patrols along the

Above: A seaplane at the Felixstowe base in 1939
Left: The view from the Fire Commander's Post. The painted images (shown in more detail in the upper photograph) depict buoys and other markers which helped to locate a target at sea

east coast and assisting in escort duties for merchant convoys. The only German attacks on Harwich and Landguard came from the air, notably in July 1917, when two bombing raids on RNAS Felixstowe resulted in seven dead and 22 wounded, and substantial material damage.

The end of the war saw a remarkable sight in the haven when some 122 vessels of the German U-boat force surrendered to Admiral Tyrwhitt. A contemporary source joyfully remarked, 'I have just witnessed one of the most wonderful sights of the war ... German U-boats being steamed up harbour under the White Ensign and with our lads in charge.'

THE SECOND WORLD WAR, 1939–45

In 1939 Harwich Haven once more became an important naval base. HMS Badger was established in Harwich, its principal role being to safeguard merchant shipping along the east coast, carried out by the Rosyth Escort Force of destroyers, minesweepers and other small vessels. Submarine flotillas also operated from the base. In 1940, HMS Beehive was established at Felixstowe Dock for torpedo boats and gun boats to escort merchant convoys and conduct offensive operations.

The Royal Navy fought with great determination to preserve the merchant shipping routes. Early in the war, German forces were laying magnetic mines along the coast to trap Allied shipping. To May 1940, mines sank 80 ships, with the loss of 600 lives. One remarkable incident took place on 21 November 1939, when a German seaplane was seen to drop parachutes within sight of Landguard; the fort was machine-gunned but the defenders, clearly surprised, did not return fire. Nothing was found during a search of the harbour entrance and six destroyers left Harwich soon after on a scheduled mission. One of them, the *Gipsy*, was broken in two after it hit a mine that had dropped by parachute from the seaplane. The ship sunk with the loss of 50 of its 150-strong crew.

Above: A British officer boarding a German U-boat at Harwich, following the surrender of the German submarine fleet in November 1918

Below: A torpedo boat based at HMS Beehive during the Second World War

In May 1940, ships of Harwich played a significant part in Operation Dynamo, the evacuation of Allied forces from Dunkirk. Harwich's naval vessels covered the evacuation and came under ferocious aerial attack. Two destroyers were sunk along with the *Waverley*, an old paddle steamer in use as a minesweeper, carrying hundreds of soldiers. Despite these losses, 6,900 troops were successfully carried back to Harwich and disembarked.

Throughout the war, Landguard Fort was the Fire Command Headquarters for the haven defences. Work began immediately to upgrade the armament, with three emplacements for twin 6-pounder guns – one at Beacon Hill (Cornwallis Battery) and two in a reconstructed Darell's Battery at Landguard. These guns, capable of extremely rapid fire, were to cover the approaches to the harbour, the beaches and the minefield. They had their own fire control towers and searchlights. The existing 6-inch guns at Landguard Right Battery and Beacon Hill were protected against aerial attack by concrete gun-houses and anti-splinter covers, while an emergency battery of two 6-inch naval guns was installed at Manor House just north of the fort. New engine rooms and searchlights were built by 1941. Extensive land defences were constructed – pillboxes, infantry trenches and barbed-wire entanglements – and the beaches and seafront were lined with tank traps and steel scaffolding barriers as obstacles to attempted landings.

In 1942 Landguard Right Battery was modified for new artillery, including two 6-inch guns that could fire at elevations up to 45°, which made them effective at long-range counter-bombardment of enemy warships. The installation of radar in 1944 enabled the guns to fire very accurately under radar control. Despite a high state of readiness, the Harwich guns opened fire only twice during the war, when friendly ships failed to give the correct recognition signal.

Above: Cleaning one of the guns at Right Battery in 1943
Below: The Little Ships at Dunkirk, by Norman Wilkinson, June 1940. Ships from Harwich played an important role in the evacuation of Allied forces

In contrast, anti-aircraft defences were kept busy. Both the naval installations and the large establishment at RAF Felixstowe were targeted by the Luftwaffe and the Italian Air Force, especially in 1940–1. Heavy anti-aircraft batteries were established on Landguard Common, and at Dovercourt, Shotley and Trimley, co-ordinated initially from headquarters in Landguard Fort. A balloon barrage was established across the entire haven, some anchored on barges in the estuary, to hinder bombing runs of enemy aircraft. At night, the searchlight crews were on several occasions machine gunned by aircraft flying down the light beams. Some 25 aircraft were brought down in the Harwich area by air and ground defences during the war.

As the war progressed, the threat to Harwich and Landguard receded. Leading up to Operation Overlord in June 1944, extensive preparations were made in Felixstowe Dock and at Landguard. When D-Day came, on 6 June, troops and tanks were embarked on landing craft and ships from three concrete hards that had been built along the riverside adjacent to Landguard Fort as part of the huge deployment. In this case, the troops and equipment formed part of the second phase of the Normandy landings.

Above and right: Posed photographs showing drill on Right Battery's number 2 6-inch gun in 1943

A Posting at Landguard

Colonel H. A. ('Dickie') Ablett recalls being posted to Landguard Fort at the beginning of the Second World War:

'I was posted to Felixstowe and Landguard in October 1939, when I was just 17. I stayed there until March 1940. There were about 12 'immatures' in my regiment at the time – chaps who were under 19 years old, the legal age for going abroad.

'In 1939 we had one of the coldest winters ever, with freezing east winds and coal rationing. My job was to prepare the pay rolls and calculate exactly what was required from the bank. The office was on the upper floor of the parade ground, and I was allowed to live there. It was terribly cold: we had fires lit for two or three hours a day until the coal ran out. We had a paliasse and bolster to sleep on – I slept on a concrete slab. We were on duty until every fifth lunchtime, 12 noon, when we were paraded and inspected before a bus took us to Ipswich for 24 hours' leave. I used to have a good bath at home – the showers at the fort were in a corrugated iron hut, where the car park is now, exposed to the weather and only for the brave.

'Late one afternoon in November 1939 a lot of parachutes were coming down in the area. We thought we were being attacked by the Germans. About half a dozen of us were sent to the top of the fort, by the Fire Command Post, as a lookout. I saw a line of destroyers coming out from Harwich: suddenly there was an almighty explosion and the third destroyer, HMS *Gipsy*, went partially down almost immediately, about half a mile offshore. The water was lit up by searchlights and there were rescue efforts from Harwich and Shotley. Later we found out that the *Gipsy* had hit a magnetic mine. Nobody had heard of these before – they were the first of Hitler's secret weapons, dropped by parachute from flying boats.'

'I saw a line of destroyers coming out from Harwich: HMS *Gipsy* went down almost immediately'

Above: Dickie Ablett (seated left) with fellow soldiers at Penlee, where he was stationed after his posting at Landguard Fort
Below: The destroyer HMS Gipsy, sunk on 21 November 1939

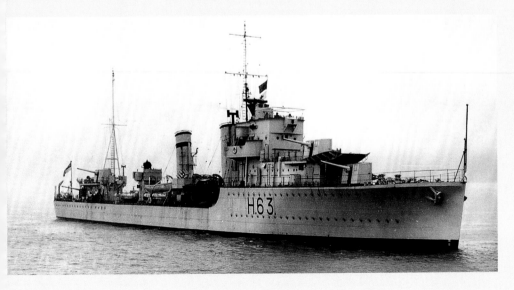

DECLINE AND DECOMMISSIONING, 1945–56

At the end of the war, the haven defences were reduced and only key installations maintained. Part of Left Battery was converted to co-ordinate the operation of six anti-aircraft batteries in the Harwich Gun Defended Area, though this closed when a purpose-built centre opened at Mistley in 1953. Similarly, the haven's coast defences were co-ordinated from a Seaward Defence Headquarters in Landguard Fort. The twin 6-pounders of Cornwallis and Darell's batteries remained in service, the latter modified to enable anti-aircraft fire from 1948. In 1956, however, all coast and anti-aircraft artillery across the nation was disbanded. Although this meant the loss of its guns, Landguard remained useful to the Army into the 1960s. Today, although its 420 years of active service have now ended, the fort is an impressive monument to the long story of coastal defence in the British Isles. It is currently managed as a visitor attraction by the Landguard Fort Trust, whose dedicated volunteers are supported by English Heritage.

Below: The Landguard peninsula today, looking north. There has been a bird observatory on the peninsula south of the fort since 1982, and the nature reserve alongside is important for many plants associated with coastal shingle